MORE BASICS IN RHYTHM

An Instructional Text

for All Instruments

by Garwood Whaley

Published By
MEREDITH MUSIC PUBLICATIONS
a division of G.W. Music, Inc.

MEREDITH MUSIC PUBLICATIONS and its stylized double M logo are trademarks
of MEREDITH MUSIC PUBLICATIONS, a division of G.W. Music, Inc.

Book layout by Jari Villanueva, J.V. Music and Tom Ginsberg
Cover design by John Heinly

ISBN: 1-57463-015-6

FOREWORD

More Basics in Rhythm, volume two of *Basics In Rhythm*, is a comprehensive collection of advanced, contemporary rhythm exercises for any instrument in individual or group instruction. The purpose of this series is to introduce and develop the rhythms and rhythmic devices common to Western art and popular music from the Renaissance to the present.

Rhythm, the fundamental element of all music, is perhaps the most troublesome aspect of musical performance. This is especially true for beginning and intermediate instrumental music students since their concentration is divided between rhythm, pitch, expression, ensemble and technical skills. By isolating rhythm and employing a system of counting, this important musical element can be learned and mastered without the interference of additional musical requirements.

This text, the continuation of rhythmic basics, provides a systematic approach to reading and understanding complex rhythm. Total mastery can be achieved through the diligent practice and application of the materials presented within. It is my sincere hope that *More Basics in Rhythm* will provide an enjoyable and educationally rewarding approach to the reading of rhythm.

G W

INTRODUCTION

More Basics in Rhythm contains eight units of advanced, contemporary rhythm exercises including syncopation, mixed meter, artificial rhythmic groups, cross-bar beaming and metric modulation. The final unit is based on composite or poly rhythms - two simultaneously played rhythms. The clapping of two rhythms together such as three against two, four against five and so forth, is an important step in developing the ability to play or conduct complex rhythms.

Each unit concludes with a rhythm duet comprised of material from that unit. The duets may be clapped by two students, teacher and student or by dividing an ensemble into two groups. These duets force the performer to concentrate on their individual part while listening to and coordinating with a rhythmically complex accompaniment. Students should be encouraged to write their own rhythmic duets as a first step towards the creative process of composition.

Practice Method

The rhythm exercises in this book are to be clapped and the syllables counted out loud. By counting out loud, the student will develop a system of "rhythm-syllable association". This system will enable the student to read rhythms at sight (regardless of the context or historical-style period). The rhythm "key" which begins each study, presents important rhythmic material and should be mastered before proceeding to the exercise that follows. Repeat each measure of the rhythm "key" at least four times, or until mastered, before proceeding to the exercise.

Note Values and Rests

Notes	Names	Rests
o	Whole	▬
♩	Half	▬
♩	Quarter	⸢
♪ (♫)	Eighth	𝄾
♪ (♬)	Sixteenth	𝄿
♪ (♬)	Thirty-second	𝅀

Notes	Names	Rests
o·	Dotted Whole	▬·
♩·	Dotted Half	▬·
♩·	Dotted Quarter	⸢·
♪·	Dotted Eighth	𝄾·
♪·	Dotted Sixteenth	𝄿·
♪·	Dotted Thirty-second	𝅀·

- A *dot* after a note or rest increases the time value of that note or rest by one-half of its original value.

  Example: ⸢· = ⸢ + ⸢   ⸢· = ⸢ + ♪

- A *second dot* after a note or rest increases the time value of the first dot by one-half of its original value.

  Example: ⸢·· = ⸢ + ⸢ + ♪   ⸢·· = ⸢ + ♪ + ♪

- A *tie* (curved line) connects two or more notes of the same pitch. Do not play (clap) the second note of a tie.

- A rhythm *triplet* occurs in music when three equal note values replace two equal note values. Additional artificial rhythmic groups include quintuplets, sextuplets, septuplets and so forth.

- In fast tempos triplets can be counted but they must be kept equal.

(Do not confuse )

- Some rhythms may be counted the same but played differently.

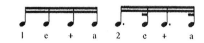

- Some rhythms, because of the number of notes, become too difficult to count in their entirety and are therefore counted using basic sub divisions only.

- Rhythms that are counted as numbers 1 2 3 4 5 6 7, once mastered, should be played without counting. Counting complex, multi-note rhythms can be difficult and may create problems.

- Some rhythms are counted alike but are not rhythmically equal.

- Metric modulation is a technique used to alter an existing pulse. At the point of change in pulse (modulation), two note values will be indicated above the staff. The first note value indicates the preceeding pulse, and the second note value indicates the new pulse. In the following example, the eighth note pulse of the 3/8 measure is equal to an eighth note of the triplet in the preceeding measure. Therefore, the pulse has been increased.

Counting Method

- Syllables in parenthesis indicate sub divisions and may be counted out loud for rhythmic security. As rhythmic mastery develops, counting parenthesized syllables may be omitted.

- When the quarter note receives one count ($\frac{2}{4}, \frac{3}{4}, \frac{4}{4}, \frac{5}{4}$ etc.), use the following measure-wise counting method (pronounced: *one an two an three an four an*):

- For the four-fold division of the beat (sixteenth notes) and its variations, use 1 e + a (pronounced: *one ee an da*):

- For the three-fold division of the beat and its variations, use 123, 456 ($\frac{6}{8}, \frac{9}{8}, \frac{12}{8}$ time when the dotted quarter note receives one count):

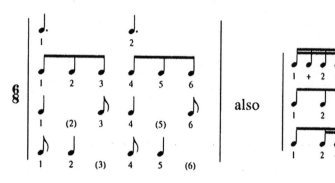

- The following examples illustrate how to count in time signatures that use the half note or eighth note as the beat unit:

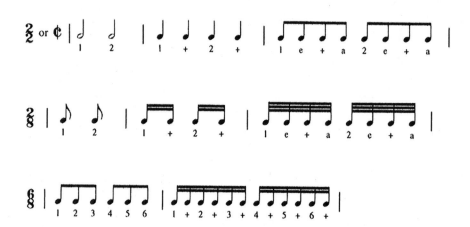

CONTENTS

UNIT 1 8

Rhythmic Device: Syncopation

Meters: ♩ ♩

Note Values: ♩ ♪. ♪ ♪

UNIT 2 13

Rhythmic Device: Dotted Rhythms

Meters: ♩ ♩ ♪

Note Values: ♩. ♩.. ♩. ♩ ♪. ♪.. ♪. ♪ ♪

UNIT 3 19

Rhythmic Device: Artificial Rhythmic Groups

Meters: ♩ ♩ ♩ ♩ ♪ ♪

Note Values: ♫ ♫ ♫ ♫ ♫ ♫ ♫

UNIT 4 25

Rhythmic Device: Complex Rhythms in Slow Tempo

Meters: ♩ ♩

Note Values: ♩ ♪ ♪ ♪

UNIT 5 31

Rhythmic Device: Changing Meters

Meters: 3 5 2 3 4 5 6 7 2 3
16 16 8 8 8 8 8 8 4 4

Note Values: ♩ ♪ ♪ ♪ ♪ ♫² ♫³ ♫⁵

UNIT 6 37

Rhythmic Device: Cross Bar Beaming

Meters: ♩ ♩ ♩ ♩

Note Values: ♩ ♪ ♪ ♫³

UNIT 7 41

Rhythmic Device: Metric Modulation

Meters: 2 3 2 3 5 6 4 5
4 4 8 8 8 8 16 16

Note Values: ♩ ♪ ♪ ♫³ ♫⁵

UNIT 8 46

Rhythmic Device: Poly Rhythms

Meters: ♩ ♩ ♩

Note Values: ♩ ♪ ♪ ♫³ ♫♫♫♫⁴

Unit 1

Rhythmic Device:	Syncopation
Meters:	$\frac{2}{4}$ $\frac{4}{4}$
Note Values:	♩ ♪. ♪ ♪

Key

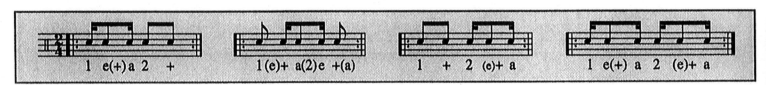

Exercise

Key

1 e(+)a 2 +   1 + a(2) e +   1 + (2) e(+)a   (1) e(+) a (2) e(+) a

Exercise

Key

1 e(+)a(2) e(+)a   (1) e(+)a(2)e(+ a)   (1) e (+ a 2)e(+ a)   (1)e (+ a) 2 +

Exercise

Key

Exercise

Key

Exercise

Key

Exercise

Duet

Unit 2

Rhythmic Device:	Dotted Rhythms
Meters:	$\frac{4}{4}$ $\frac{2}{4}$ $\frac{6}{8}$
Note Values:	𝅗𝅥. 𝅗𝅥.. ♩. ♩ ♪. ♪.. ♪. ♪ 𝅘𝅥𝅯

Key

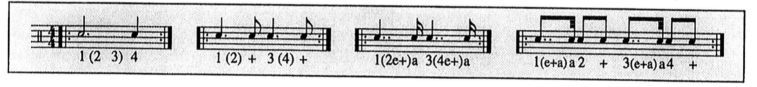

Exercise

14

Key

Exercise

Key

Exercise

Key

1(2)+3 4 5 6

1 2(3)+4 5 6

1(2)+ 3 4 5(6)+

1 2 (3)+ 4(5) + 6

Exercise

Key

1 2 +3 +4 5 6

1 +2 +3 4 5 6

1 2 +3 +4 +5 +6

1 +2 +3 4 5 +6 +

Exercise

17

Key

Exercise

Key

Exercise

18

Duet

Unit 3

Rhythmic Device:	**Artificial Rhythmic Groups**
Meters:	$\frac{2}{4}\ \frac{3}{4}\ \frac{4}{4}\ \frac{5}{4}\ \frac{6}{4}\ \frac{6}{8}$
Note Groups:	*2 3 4 5 6 7*

Key

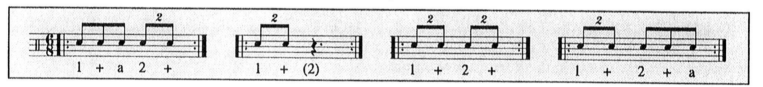

Exercise

Key

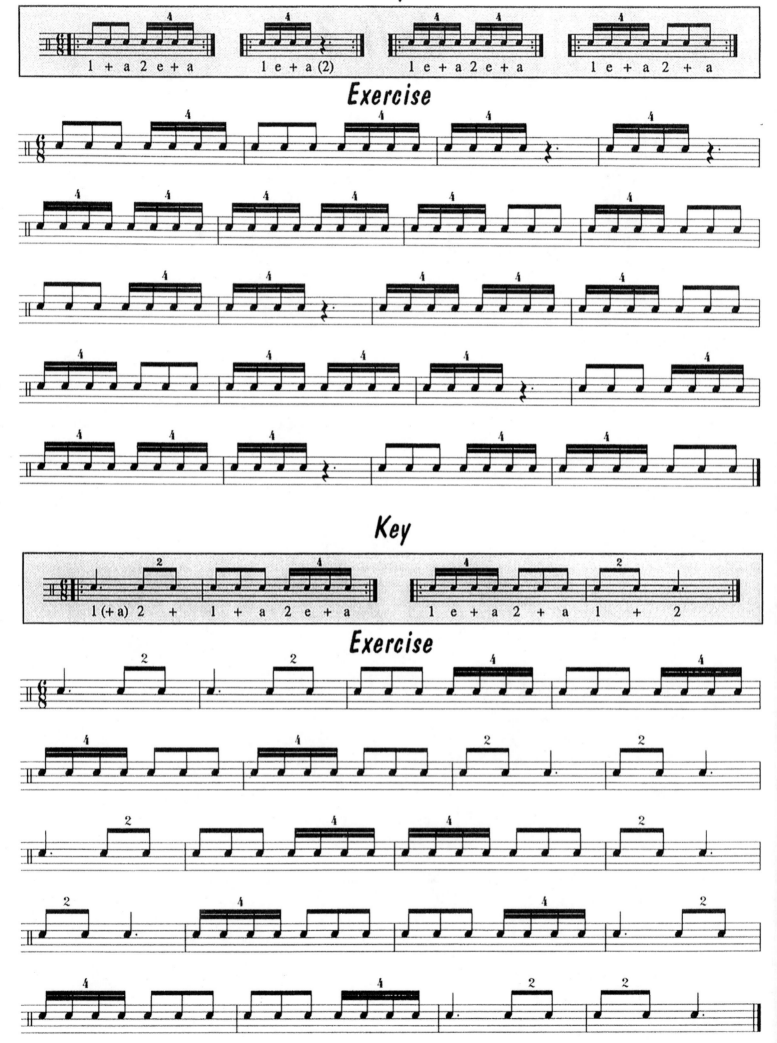

1 + a 2 e + a   1 e + a (2)   1 e + a 2 e + a   1 e + a 2 + a

Exercise

Key

1 (+ a) 2 +   1 + a 2 e + a   1 e + a 2 + a 1 + 2

Exercise

Key

Exercise

Key

Exercise

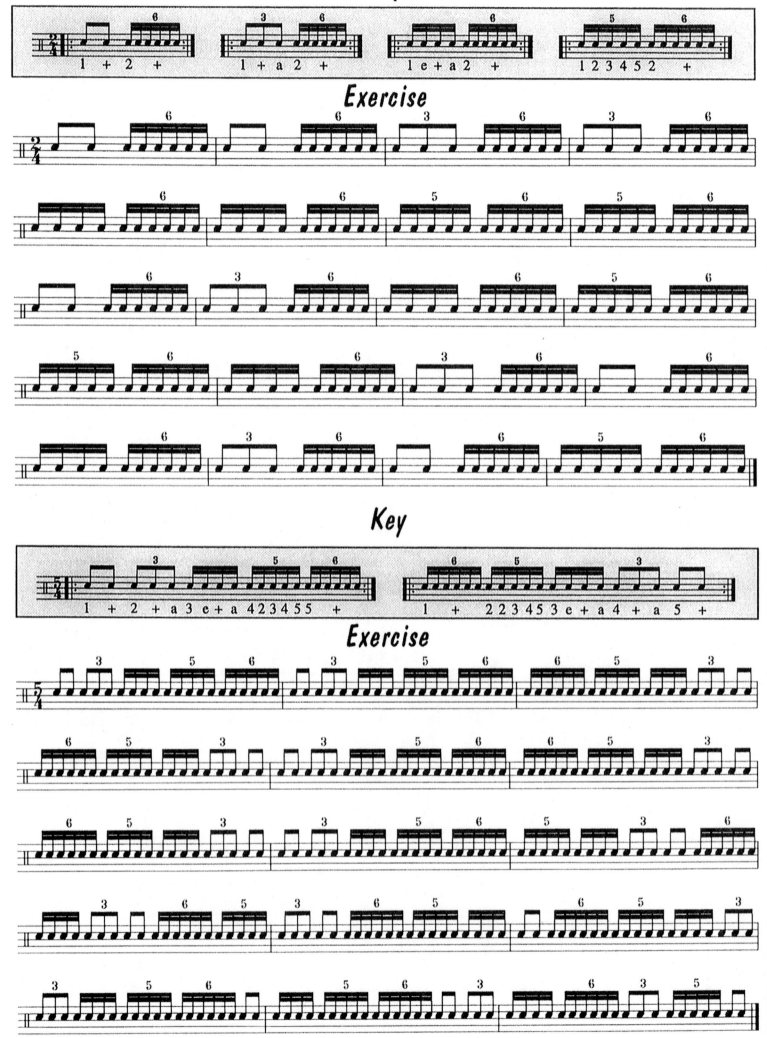

23

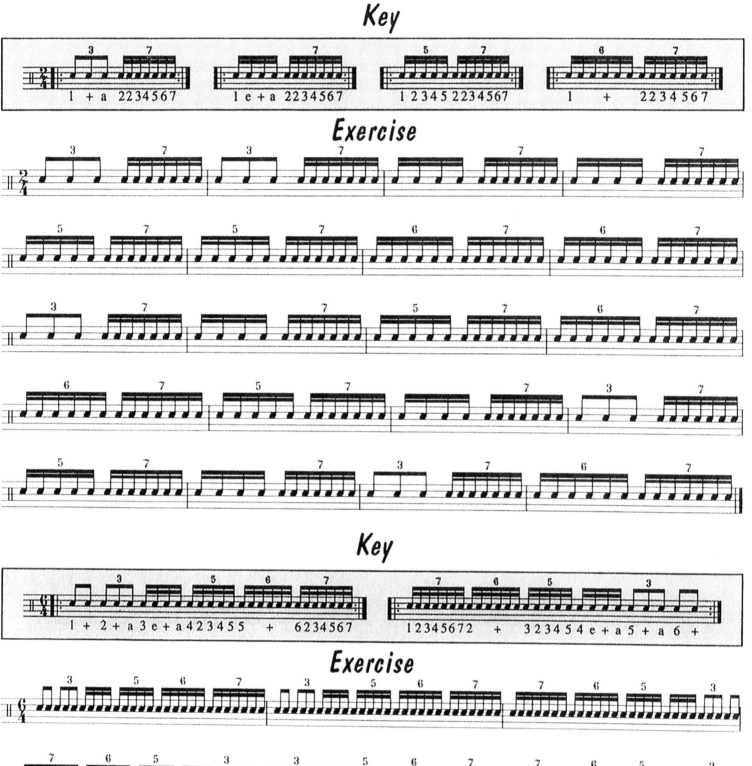

Duet

Unit 4

Rhythmic Device: **Complex Rhythms**
in Slow Tempo

Meters: $\frac{2}{4}$ $\frac{3}{4}$

Note Values: ♩ ♪ ♫ ♬

Key

(slow tempo ca. ♩ = 60)

Exercise

26

Key

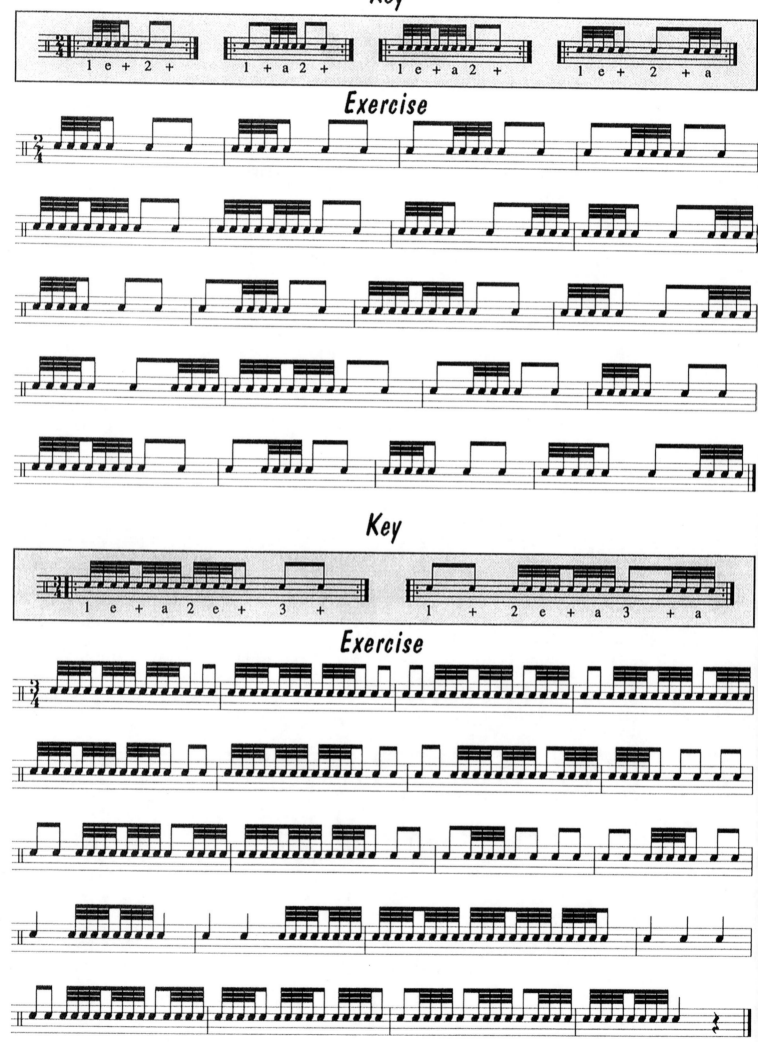

Exercise

Key

Exercise

Key

Exercise

Key

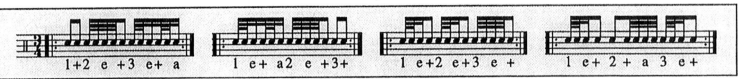

Exercise

28

Key

Exercise

Key

Exercise

Key

Exercise

Key

Exercise

Duet

Unit 5

Rhythmic Device:	Changing Meters
Meters:	3/16 5/16 2/8 3/8 4/8 5/8 6/8 7/8 2/4 3/4
Note Values:	♩ ♪ ♪ ♪ ♫ ♬ ♬

Key

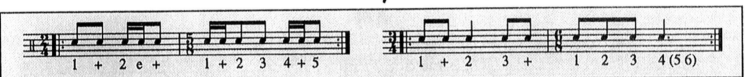

Exercise

Key

Exercise

Key

Exercise

Key

Exercise

Key

Exercise

Duet

Unit 6

Rhythmic Device:	Cross Bar Beaming
Meters:	$\frac{2}{4}$ $\frac{2}{8}$ $\frac{3}{8}$ $\frac{5}{8}$
Note Values:	♩ ♪ ♪ (triplet)

Key

Exercise

Key

Exercise

Key

Exercise

Duet

Unit 7

Rhythmic Device:	Metric Modulation
Meters:	$\frac{2}{4}$ $\frac{3}{4}$ $\frac{2}{8}$ $\frac{3}{8}$ $\frac{5}{8}$ $\frac{6}{8}$ $\frac{4}{16}$ $\frac{5}{16}$
Note Values:	♩ ♪ 𝅘𝅥𝅮 (triplet 3) (quintuplet 5)

Key

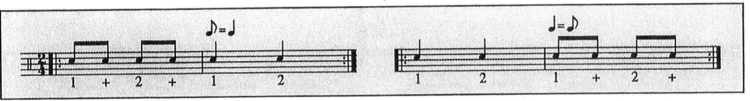

Exercise

42

Key

Exercise

Key

Exercise

Key

Exercise

Key

Exercise

Duet

Unit 8

Rhythmic Device:	Poly Rhythms
Meters:	$\frac{2}{4}$ $\frac{3}{4}$ $\frac{5}{4}$
Note Values:	♩ ♪ ♪ 3 JJJ 4 JJJJ

Key

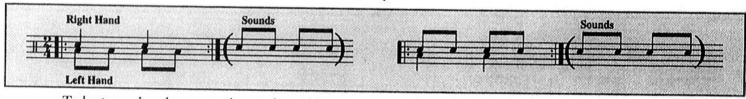

To be tapped on leg or music stand or table etc.

Exercise

Key

Exercise

Key

Exercise